# If You Give a Boy a Bible

by Andy Holmes

# If You Give a Boy a Bible

## Bible

by Andy Holmes

KREGEL Kidzone
Where Kids are number One

*If You Give a Boy a Bible*

© 2004 by Andy Holmes

Published by Kregel Kidzone, an imprint of Kregel Publications, P.O. Box 2607, Grand Rapids, MI 49501.

All rights reserved.

ISBN 0-8254-5513-8

Printed in China

**If you give a boy a Bible . . .**

He may ask you
to read it to him.

While you're
reading it to him,
he may want to sit
on your lap . . .

or lie on your
back . . .

or hang upside down,
halfway on the couch
and halfway off.

**When you get to a story with a fight scene . . .**

he may want to
act it out.

He may make up his
own ending.

Then, just when you think you're
safe, he may want to act it out all
over again.

He may feel sad when you read the part where Adam and Eve disobey God.

**When you read a story about Bible bandits,
you might need to keep a close watch
over your shish kebabs.**

He may act like a baboon when
he discovers the story of Noah
and the floating zoo.

**Hearing that Joseph's brothers sold him to a group of travelers from a distant land . . .**

may give him new
temptations to overcome.

After you read
him the story
about Moses
and the ten
plagues . . .

he's likely to collect frogs for a month!

And the "Moses crossing the Red Sea" story may inspire him . . .

**to try a red Kool-Aid experiment
in your neighbor's hot tub.**

Once he learns the story of Balaam and
his talking donkey . . .

he may try to interview his
iguana, Izzie.

After you read him
the story of Rahab and
Joshua's two spies . . .

**you may never have a private
moment again.**

# Tip: If you have a tuba in the house . . .

skip the story about Joshua blowing
the walls of Jericho down.

If you give a boy a Bible, he may learn to be calm when the night light goes out . . .

be kind to others even when they are mean to him . . .

and learn to trust a Friend who's there when no one else is.

If you give a boy a Bible, he just may discover that a great big, wonderful God loves him more than he could ever imagine.

Who knows? Maybe after reading him the story of how Daniel and his young friends turned down a king's feast for veggies, he may actually want to try broccoli for himself . . .

or maybe not.

But he may want to share these
stories with a friend.

And if he shares the stories . . .

he may want to give that boy a Bible, too!